PIGTAIL PILOT

The brief life of
aviator Barbara Gubbins

by BILL TODD

PIGTAIL PILOT

First published as an ebook and paperback in 2015 by
DLE-History - www.billtodd.co.uk

Copyright ©BillTodd 2015

The moral right of Bill Todd to be identified as the author of this work has been asserted by him in accordance with the Copyright, Designs and Patents Act 1988.
All rights reserved. No part of this publication may be reproduced, stored in or introduced into a retrieval system, or transmitted, in any form, or by any means (electronic, mechanical, photocopying, recording or otherwise) without the prior written permission of the publisher. Any person who does any unauthorised act in relation to this publication may be liable to criminal prosecution and civil claims for damages. This book is sold subject to the condition that it shall not, by way of trade or otherwise, be lent, re-sold, hired out, or otherwise circulated without the publisher's prior consent in any form of binding or cover other than that in which it is published and without a similar condition including this condition being imposed on the subsequent purchaser.

***

BILL TODD is the author of the DANNY LANCASTER series of crime thriller novels. PIGTAIL PILOT is the second in his history series, following publication of GUNNER, the story is his father's service in World War Two. For more details, visit:

WEBSITE: www.billtodd.co.uk
FACEBOOK: www.facebook.com/DannyLancasterInvestigates
TWITTER: https://twitter.com/williamjtodd

THE LAST DAY
A 17-minute flight

The training flight took off at 11.40am. The instructor, Flight Lieutenant Eric Church, was a 31-year-old veteran of Coastal Command in World War Two, mentioned in despatches for "valuable services in the air".

His pupil was 20-year-old Barbara Gubbins, a Royal Air Force Volunteer Reserve trainee pilot who had already logged 150 flying hours.

The aircraft, a single-engine, two-seater Percival Prentice Mk1 of 16 Reserve Flying School, took off from RAF Burnaston near Derby and headed westward over the open farming country of south Derbyshire.

The aim of the day was the practice the recognition and recovery from a spin, a vital element of training to enable a pilot to recover when their aircraft loses lift and control and spirals earthwards like a leaf.

Seventeen minutes after takeoff the aircraft spun into the ground just north of the River Dove near the village of Scropton.

The crew might have attempted to bail out but both were killed when the Prentice hit the ground.

Barbara Gubbins lived for flying and was close to becoming the first qualified woman pilot in the Royal Air Force.

But Barbara was also a talented horse rider, accomplished sportswoman and passionate about science. At a time when glass ceilings were probably lower than they are now, she reached for the sky.

Barbara's school magazine described her with words like "zest", "unswerving determination", "outstanding achievement", "exceptionally able", "infectious interest". And these words were more than 60 years ago when praise was harder to come by.

She strikes me as an exceptional young woman. She was also my cousin. I never met her but have always felt her achievement and lost potential should be remembered.

Here is Barbara's story.

BILL TODD

PIGTAIL PILOT

PIGTAIL PILOT: Barbara was always distinguished by her braided hair as illustrated in this photo from a newspaper. The caption on a photo taken by a nation picture agency dubbed her the "Pigtail Pilot" because her hair was coiled under her flying helmet

THE CRASH
Just another training flight

Percival Prentice Mk1 VS 645 came down in a field near Foston Hall Woods, off Leathersley Lane, Scropton, a mile east of Sudbury Station, on Wednesday March 5, 1952.

The Derby Telegraph reported that day that the unfolding tragedy was first spotted by two boys from Scropton Hall Approved School which is now a women's prison that has housed Maxine Carr and Moors murderer Myra Hindley.

The boys noticed the aircraft's wing dipping and alerted a teacher. After the aircraft hit, the boys and a teacher ran to the crash site with a stretcher and blankets. Farm workers who were baling hay came

from the Derby Telegraph. You can see the effect of the spinning manoeuvre from the way the aircraft has twisted into the ground

running from surrounding fields. They found Flt Lt Church in the cockpit and Barbara on the ground nearby.

Both were dead but they moved Flt Lt Church's body in case the aircraft caught fire. Fortunately, it didn't.

Eyewitnesses reported that the canopy doors had been jettisoned as the aircraft came down and it appeared Barbara may have attempted to bail out which might explain why she was found outside the aircraft.

Fire crews, police and ambulance staff came to the scene from Burton and Derby. The bodies were taken to Hatton mortuary and the Army posted a guard at the crash site.

The Nottingham Evening Post reported that Barbara had been lodged in Pelham Crescent, The Park, Nottingham. Landlady Mrs Mason said: "It is a terrible shock to us. She was a really loveable girl. It will be a great blow to her parents. She was an only child."

A FLYING START
But one or two unfortunate lapses in conduct

From the age of ten, Barbara Gubbins was passionate about flying. She saved up for lessons by picking fruit and giving riding lessons and flew solo at the age of 17 after just 5½ hours training.

Although flying was her great love she was also a talented horsewoman and enjoyed rifle shooting, hockey and tennis.

Barbara Mary Gubbins was born on April 9, 1931 in West Wycombe Road, High Wycombe.

Her birth certificate lists her mother's full name as Edith Annie Mabel Gubbins nee Jeffries, who became headmistress of Hedsor village school in Buckinghamshire. She was always known to the family as "Mabs".

Barbara's father was Valentine Owen Gubbins, a police sergeant with Buckinghamshire Constabulary – now Thames Valley – who was stationed at Great Missenden Police Office. He later worked as an animal inspector.

His Gubbins line can trace the family back to William of Byfield, a farmer in 1600s Northamptonshire. The family lived in nearby Chipping Warden for some 300 years up to the early 1900s.

After attending Green Street School, Barbara moved up to Wycombe High School where she started on September 9, 1941, joining Hampden House. Her mother Mabs had been a pupil from 1918 to 1924.

Wycombe High School opened in 1901 with 18 students and three staff in a building known today as Clock House in Frogmoor, High Wycombe.

The school moved to Benjamin Road in 1906 where it remained for 50 years except during the First World War when it was transferred to the old grammar school while its buildings were used as a military hospital.

By 1922 there were 300 pupils and by 1956 demand was so great that the school moved to the present site on Marlow Hill.

Wycombe High School girls' grammar now has approximately 1,340 pupils age 11 to 18 and became an academy in 2011.

The glowing tributes to Barbara's skills and ambitions after her death were fully justified but eulogies, whoever they are for, are always relentlessly positive. With limited research material it is difficult to penetrate into the mind behind the smiling, plait-framed face in the family's old photos.

But Barbara's school reports from Wycombe High give something of an insight into her early life and character. Written in the days before allowances were made for sensitive pupils and anxious ambitious parents, they give a little colour and shade to the black and white photos. Frustratingly, they also pose new questions that the available research materials do not answer.

Her report card for that autumn records 20 absences and adds she "appears to resent criticism"... "should try to remedy faults."

The spring 1942 entry reports Barbara, "Has been a more cheerful member of form" but adds she "is inclined to rely too much on facts and not use her reasoning powers".

In autumn 1942 her progress has been, "good in spite of absence" and records 35 absences with no gym or games due to an accidental fracture. In spring 1943 she has been, "Good, useful, but must not be a law to herself." There were 16 absences.

In autumn 1943 teachers say Barbara, "finds it difficult to cooperate with her form" and "But must avoid inaccuracy and untidy presentation".

TEAM PLAYER: Barbara in the Wycombe High School hockey first eleven team 1949-50. She is to the right of the girl wearing pads

There is a slight change of tone in the report for summer 1944 – "Barbara's attitude has been more friendly this term" and her exam results show "creditable progress" but adds "there have been one or two unfortunate lapses in conduct".

In autumn 1944 she is "public spirited and considerate" and in spring 1945, "can be very helpful when she wishes".

Barbara's independent-mindedness is highlighted again in her report for autumn 1945 which says, "She is inclined to work only when the spirit moves her" and adds "This low grade in English is inexcusable". There were 14 absences.

In autumn 1945 Barbara, "could achieve A grade in most subjects" but in spring 1946 is, "handicapped by inability to express herself on paper". By that summer she had, "made a pleasing effort this term" and was a, "very good member of the Puppet Club, excellent at lighting effects".

In autumn 1946 Barbara is, "always ready to take an active part in class discussion but she does not show enthusiasm for written work".

In spring 1947 Barbara's teachers expressed the concern that her early decision to focus on maths and sciences could lead to, "a one-sided intellectual development" and adds "B must not adopt the idea that art subjects are neither real nor significant".

The reports make clear that by now Barbara is clearly a young woman of talent with a single-mindedness that might border on the stubborn in the view of teachers aiming for a broad and balanced education.

Autumn 1947 reports Barbara as the, "enthusiastic president of the science club," that the club's success is mostly due to her work and that she has shown talent herself. Spring 1948 adds, "Barbara is certainly justifying her choice of chemistry".

In summer 1948 her progress is described as, "very good – Barbara has been a valuable reliable prefect. Her work is very good" and bodes "well for the future".

Under 'remarks' it says, "Prefect. Solo flight in five hours. Top in senior school in chemistry. This is work of a high quality. Barbara is making history".

The autumn 1948 report reads, "In spite of home difficulties B has shown her usual cheerfulness. Her achievement in chemistry is excellent but she must support this with high performance in her other subjects". Under 'remarks' it adds, "Games captain. Gained pilot's licence. Father broke leg".

The rollercoaster of Barbara's school life takes a bit of a dip in spring 1949, "B continues to do good work particularly in chemistry but she will fail to achieve her highest results unless her English improves. Her inability to express ideas clearly will be a constant handicap. Barbara must find time for wider reading if she wishes to be regarded as well educated".

And summer 1949, "Barbara has worked well but we hope that next year it will be possible for her to concentrate all her energy and attention upon the development of her work. As a prefect she has taken an active and helpful interest in school affairs. It will require a total effort on B's part next year if she is to achieve entrance to London University in these difficult days."

In autumn 1949 she has, "worked very well... tackled a new subject with vigour... raised the general level of her work".

In spring 1950 Barbara has, "a very good level of work. B contributes a great deal to the form by her energy and keen interest in school affairs", but in summer 1950, the last entry, "Barbara has had a very anxious year".

Her final report card shows her exams as B grades for English Language, Latin and domestic science, A-minus for history, geography and gym and As for algebra, geometry, applied mathematics, chemistry and games. Her overall pass mark was A-minus. She left Wycombe High on July 27, 1950.

So, the school reports paint a patchy picture of a young woman with talent, determination and weakness in certain areas who single-mindedly pursues her own interests and passions, sometime in the teeth of advice from others.

One school contemporary described her as, "A larger-than-life person, but a bit over the top."

They added that her father doted on her and, after the fatal crash, broke down in tears whenever her name was mentioned.

Although the school reports shade in Barbara's picture a little they leave intriguing questions. Barbara was a keen horsewoman. Was that the cause of her accidental fracture? What were the "unfortunate lapses in conduct"?

Why was her English grade "inexcusable" when she was the daughter of a teacher? What were the "home difficulties"? And why was her last year "very anxious"?

It would be fascinating to know the answer to these and other mysteries but it would be unfair to speculate. This is an object lesson is asking your family questions while those who witnessed these events are still alive and able to answer.

In addition to her passion for science at school Barbara was an accomplished sportswoman. She was school games captain and Hockey 1st XI captain 1949-50, captain of the tennis 2nd XI in 1949 and played hockey for the county.

The school magazine records her playing right half in the school Hockey team 1st XI in autumn 1947. The comments on her play reads, "She is a very hard worker and has good anticipation although she is sometimes slow in recovery."

I felt a slight shiver when I read that, picturing an aircraft trying to break out of a spin too close to the ground.

SPORTY: Barbara, pictured in the front row, fourth from the left, was Wycombe school's games captain in 1949

Barbara's competitive nature extended to winning a book prize as part of a school general competition in summer 1947.

The contest included identifying butterflies, flowers and birds' eggs, an electrical test to make a bell ring, identifying liquids and powders by smell, designing a bike and seeing who could suck the most water up a capillary tube in one breath.

She did not spurn the arts entirely as the summer 1945 edition of the school magazine includes her review of the Wycombe High's production of Thackeray's The Rose And The Ring.

Barbara features in a home movie clip taken at a party in the late 1940s in the garden of her school friend Margaret Cayzer. There is a table of post-war party food on the ration and the girls are playing on a swing.

And Barbara still plays a small part in the life of Wycombe High School today with the annual presentation of The Barbara Gubbins Senior Chemistry Prize.

SMILING SCHOLAR: Barbara with her parents at Nottingham University where she studied chemistry

PIGTAIL PILOT

The school magazine says, "Barbara was a pupil from 1942-49. She did brilliantly in chemistry at Higher School Certificate.

"When she was in the Sixth form, no chemistry teacher could be found, and three times a week the WHS chemists had to walk to the RGS (Royal Grammar School) for their lessons.

"Barbara was killed in an air crash two years after she left school. This prize is awarded to the student whose class work has consistently been of the highest standard – it is not to be awarded on the basis of exam results."

Barbara's mother is also remembered with the annual presentation of The Mabel Gubbins Senior Biology Prize to the student whose class work has consistently been of the highest standard achieved, not on exam results.

Barbara was a member of Wycombe Young Farmers Club and after her death her parents instituted the Barbara Gubbins Award presented annually for the best essay on the theme of the preservation of the countryside. The winner was presented with a shield by Mabs.

Barbara went on to study for an honours degree in chemistry, pure maths and physics at Nottingham University. She had flown solo from Denham Airfield at the age of 17 after just 5½ hours training and qualified for her private pilot's licence soon after.

She flew regularly with Denham Aero Club and High Wycombe Flying Club and at one time was Britain's youngest female pilot. In 1949 she took her mother Mabs up in a Piper Cub from Denham to cruise over their home at Hedsor.

Barbara celebrated her 20th birthday with an "air battle" when she and 10 other pilots defended Denham Airfield against 20 "attacking" aircraft.

The manager of Denham Aero Club told a newspaper: "We challenged other clubs to get planes to the airfield without being spotted. They must come in between 1,000 and 2,000 feet and our aircraft will be patrolling. Pilots and crews who get through will be given a free breakfast."

PIGTAIL PILOT

When Barbara was photographed by a national photo agency the image was captioned "Pigtailed Pilot" as he wore her braided hair coiled up under her flying helmet.

In 1951 she was a guest on the radio celebrity chat show In Town Tonight which, during its long history, also featured Errol Flynn, Gary Cooper, Jane Russell and Doris Day.

Barbara joined the Women's Royal Air Force Volunteer Reserve and trained weekly at Burnaston for 18 months before her death, logging more than 150 hours in the air including night flights.

A letter from Nottingham University to the chief training officer at the Bristol Aeroplane Company says Barbara had, "The makings of a really able pilot. She certainly knows more about aircraft engines, principles of flight and so on than the keenest ATC (Air Training Corps) boy".

Aviation history is full of women pioneers, from Amy Johnson, who set numerous long-distance records, to the pilots of the ATA (Air Transport Auxiliary) who ferried aircraft in the Second World War. Cadet Pilot 2674733 Barbara Gubbins was believed to be the youngest pilot in the WRAFVR.

If she had lived, she might well have been the first woman awarded RAF wings. That distinction went just six months later to Pilot Officer Jean Lennox Bird.

CHOCKS AWAY: Barbara in the cockpit of an unidentified aircraft

CRASH INQUIRY
Failure of the human element

An inquest into the Scropton crash was held two days later on March 7 at Hatton Village Hall by Arthur Whiston, coroner for south Derbyshire.

The Derby Telegraph reported that Burnaston's chief instructor, Squadron Leader Findlay, told the inquest Flt Lt Church was a very experienced pilot, flying since 1939, and that Barbara had approximately 150 hours flying, and was, "very capable and had the makings of a competent pilot."

He added, "She was a very good pilot and had flown solo. This was just another training flight. They go on for a long time after a pilot has made their first solo flight."

Sqn Ldr Findlay added that he had seen Flt Lt Church at between 10am and 10.30am and they took off at 11.40.

Eyewitness Raymond Harris, 47, a farm worker of Heath Way, Hatton, said he was in Scropton at 11.50am when he saw "a plane over Foston Woods. It was just spinning down."

He added that he saw a lot of training aircraft and thought this one slightly lower than normal. He was standing by a tractor with its engine running so could not hear the aircraft's engine although it did not appear to be power diving. He saw the aircraft spinning down "slightly nose first".

"I watched the crash after seeing the plane spinning in the air. With some other men with whom I had been baling hay in the next field I rushed to the plane and pulled the instructor free in case there should be a fire."

Mr Harris saw the canopy panels fly off at about 400 feet and added that the aircraft was still spinning when it hit. He ran to the aircraft with a workmate and found Barbara a short distance from the aircraft. Fl Lt Church was face down on the wing.

Brian Bullen of Firs Farm said the spin appeared normal although the aircraft seemed low. At about 350 feet he saw the canopy doors fall away. At about 200 feet he saw someone stand up in the aircraft but lost sight of them. The aircraft was still spinning when it hit the ground nose first.

The coroner recalled Sqn Ldr Findlay who said that the crew should have been strapped in and that if anyone attempted to stand up it would appear they were trying to abandon the aircraft.

Kenneth Fells, chief engineer of Airscrew Ltd, the company responsible for the operation of No16 Flying School, told the inquest that the aircraft, which had side-by-side dual-controls, was inspected and certified airworthy on the morning of the crash.

He had inspected the aircraft, manufactured in October 1947, after the crash and did not find any mechanical defect.

Dr Geoffrey Abbey of Tutbury said both victims had fractured skulls which would have caused instant death.

The coroner recorded verdicts of accidental death.

Barbara's death certificate, dated March 8, described her as a "spinster university student" and "daughter of Valentine Owen Gubbins, inspector of diseases of animals London County Council" of Harvest Hill, Bourne End, Bucks.

It gave the cause of death as, "Fracture of the base of the skull accidentally caused when the aeroplane in which she was riding crashed to the ground." No post mortem was held. The certificate is signed by Sophia Wilson, registrar of Hatton sub district of Derbyshire.

IMPACT POINT: The field near Foston Woods where the aircraft crashed   Picture: PAT CUNNINGHAM

The accident report of April 21, 1952, from the RAF court of inquiry concluded the crash was caused by "a failure of the human element" as there was no mechanical failure and no evidence to explain why the aircraft was spinning below the authorised height.

The report, headed "RAFVR refresher (Demonstrating spinning)" records that the aircraft took off at 11.40am and crashed 17 minutes later. It places the wreck at 080 degrees, one miles east of Sudbury Station.

The report says: "A/C (aircraft) was seen by two civilian witnesses spinning towards the ground from about 400ft.

"At about 300ft the cabin canopy was jettisoned and the rate of rotating slowed down as the spirals became wider. A/C finally struck the ground and both occupants were thrown from A/C.

"The court considered that in the absence of any technical fault the accident must be ascribed to a failure of the human element. There was no evidence to show why the A/C was spinning below the authorised height."

The Scropton incident features in the book *White Peak Air Crash Sites by* Pat Cunningham DFM, an air crash historian and aviator of 40 years' experience with 20,000 hours of military and commercial flying.

Pat wrote, "Flight Lieutenant Church's detail was to further familiarise his pupil with the complexities of spinning, essentially an out-of-control revolution.

"Contemporary rules demanded that practice spins should be entered at a minimum of 5,000 feet above ground level (AGL). The guidance read, 'when you have come down to 3,000 feet, you must prepare to abandon …be sure… that you can be out of the aircraft by 1,000 feet'."

Pat added, "This was not to be the last spinning fatality but certainly it helped raised awareness of this facet of flight safety for shortly afterwards the rules would state unequivocally, 'If spin recovery action has not been effective by 3,000 feet AGL, abandon the aircraft'."

Retired Group Captain RB Gubbins, no direct relation, said, "The photographic evidence of Barbara's crash site shows a very flat attitude on impact."

Gp Capt Gubbins, who had many years experience as a flying instructor and later served on the teaching staff of the RAF Staff College, added, "It looks to me as if they clearly had settled into a well-developed flat spin from which it would extremely difficult to recover without an enormous loss of altitude as the aircraft must be made to first pitch nose down so that airflow over the elevators and rudder may resume and the spin my become a normal nose-down spin which will then respond to the usual spin recovery procedure."

THE AFTERMATH
Much achievement in a short life

The Wycombe High School magazine recorded Barbara's death in the summer 1952 issue under the headline "Barbara Gubbins, 1941-1950". It said:

"It was with a great feeling of sorrow that we at school learnt of the death of Barbara in a flying accident.

"At first we were filled with a sense of the untimeliness of her death but we are beginning to realise how much there was of achievement in her short life.

"Even as a little girl in the 1st form she was interested in flying and this was the subject she often chose to write about in her compositions. This interest she pursued with unswerving determination and she made her first solo flight when she was seventeen.

"In other ways Barbara was outstanding. For two years she was an exceptionally able games captain and some of us will remember her zest for the gymnastic competition and how, with her infectious interest, she swept the most unlikely Upper VIth girls into practising for this event.

"We remember her love of horses and how at home she seemed to feel with all animals.

"Barbara early showed interest and real ability in the science classes. She was a keen experimenter. One pictures her arrival at the laboratory one day during her last school year, all set to carry out an experiment of which she had read, her flourish of the test tube and remark of sheer delight, "Look, it really works!"

"The school took pride in Barbara's achievements in scholarship and games but particularly in the courage which made her able to qualify so early to fly alone. As a daughter of an Old Girl and a pupil here for nine years, Barbara was very much a child of the School and she will be remembered with pride and affection."

The wife of a tutor at Nottingham University described Barbara as, "A most attractive and popular girl and an outstanding personality."

HONOUR GUARD
Hundreds attend the funeral

In an age before health and safety inquiries and compensation claims events moved more quickly.

Following the crash on Wednesday March 5, 1952, Barbara was cremated in Nottingham on March 8 and the funeral was held at Hedsor Parish Church on March 12.

Hundreds of mourners attended a service conducted by the Rev E P Horton, Vicar of Hedsor, assisted by the Rev A W Jayne, Vicar of Little Marlow. Chief mourners were Mr and Mrs V O Gubbins and Mrs H J Jeffries, Barbara's grandmother.

Mourners included representatives from Nottingham University Air Squadron, High Wycombe Riding Club, Denham Flying Club and High Wycombe High School.

The Bucks Free Press reported that there were 88 floral tributes, many in the shape of propellers and wings, including ones from Nottingham University Chemistry Department, No16 Flying School Derby, officers and airmen of No 65 Reserve Centre Alverston, Nottingham University Air Squadron, staff and pupils of Hedsor School, British Railways Maidenhead, Bourne End School, Denham Flying Club, Wycombe Flying Club, Marlow Hockey Club, High Wycombe High School, The Head Teachers' Association, WRAFVR Burnaston, Nottingham University Rifle Club and High Wycombe Riding School.

Barbara's ashes were buried in the church graveyard at Hedsor. As the casket was interred two RAF officers who had escorted it from RAF Cardington saluted at the graveside.

Sometime later one of Barbara's closest school friends had her wedding bouquet laid on the gravestone.

Today the memorial sandstone set flat in the grass beside her parents' grave is weather-worn and sunken, the lettering almost impossible to read.

But Hedsor Parish Church stands high on a hill looking out on a sweeping panorama across the River Thames and the Chiltern hills.

It is a real pilot's eye view.

PEOPLE, PLACES AND PLANES

MABS GUBBINS

Barbara's mother was born Edith Annie Mabel Jeffries on April 5, 1906, and attended Green Street Elementary School.

She then went up to Wycombe High School where records give her address as Kitchener Road, High Wycombe, and her father's occupation as time and store keeper at an electric power plant.

Edith, always known to her family as Mabs, began her studies at WHS on September 19, 1918, and left in July 1924.

Her final report card said she had, "worked very well throughout the term and has shown judgement and common sense" although it did record two absences and one lateness.

Mabs became a student teacher, training at St Gabriel's College in Camberwell, South London, and went on to teach at Mill End School in High Wycombe, now Millbrook Combined School. She married in 1928.

The log books for Hedsor School held at the Centre For Bucks Studies show that Mabs took up her duties as headmistress at Hedsor School in Harvest Hill on December 1, 1943. Her Assistant was Miss E Winch.

The small school had a close family atmosphere. One pupil who was taught by Mabs says, "I remember the Christmas Nativity scene that was in the 'big' classroom. I even remember how strange it seemed to be in your classroom at night as that was when the children and parents would go to see it.

"I clearly remember the carol concerts at Hedsor Church, too, and that long uphill walk on a frosty December night.

"It was this concert that meant Christmas had 'started' as generally it was held on the evening of the day the school had broken up for Christmas.

"I remember too that we used to have plays held in the church hall in Wooburn Green opposite Soho paper mill, long gone now."

Another pupil writes, "I was a pupil at Hedsor School and I remember Mrs Gubbins very well. Memories of that wonderful little school are a treasure to look back on. I remember we used to have lunch sometimes on the green opposite the school in the summer months. Just to stand in what was the playground would bring memories flooding back. I can remember the van that used to deliver the lunch from Bourne End. It was driven by a Mr Whitehead. On his last day we tied him to the van!"

The school was built by George Ives Irby, 4th Baron Boston (1802-1869) in 1858. His home was Hedsor House, a Georgian-style mansion overlooking the Thames.

There has been a manor house at Hedsor since 1166. The current building featured in the 2012 Dustin Hoffman film Quartet starring Maggie Smith and Michael Gambon and Mortdecai (2015) starring Johnny Depp, Olivia Munn, and Paul Bettany.

Mabs spent most of her professional career as head at Hedsor School and when she retired it closed and became a private house.

Mabs moved to a beautiful cottage in West Lane, Bledlow, near Chinnor, not far from her old school. She died on March 26, 1986.

I never had the opportunity to meet Barbara, my second cousin. I did have the privilege of knowing Mabs and have fond memories of visiting her in retirement in Bledlow.

Serious medical problems never dented Mabs' joy in meeting new people, trundling down to the village pub in her wheelchair for lunch and enjoying a G&T.

To the end of her life she was bright and lively with a mischievous sense of humour, telling stories in her broad Bucks accent.

Meeting Mabs, it was not hard to see where Barbara inherited her energy, determination and zest for life.

VAL GUBBINS

Barbara's father was born Valentine Owen Gubbins in 1902. His family came from the villages of Chipping Warden and Edgcote north east of Banbury.

The Battle of Edgcote in the Wars of the Roses was fought there in July 1469. The family line in this part of Northamptonshire goes back to William Gubbins, born around 1600.

The surname often raises a smile. It is defined as, "General clutter, stuff, a collection or assortment of unconnected items" as in "He had a lot of gubbins in his bag".

It appears to originate from the family named Gobion(s) who came over with the Norman invasion of England in 1066 or soon afterwards and received grants of land located mainly in Essex, Herts, Beds and Northants.

The name spread to Ireland and around the world. It is the subject of research by Gp Capt Gubbins, a member of the Guide Of One-Name Studies. Val joined Buckinghamshire Constabulary, now part of Thames Valley Police, on May 28, 1923, and was given the collar number 30.

In his application he is described as 21 3/12ths, five feet ten inches tall, with brown hair and grey eyes. It adds he was born at Culworth Mill, Chipping Warden, a schoolteacher by trade and last employed by W J Gubbins, his father.

As a policeman, his pay was 70 shillings (£3.50) a week. By 1935 this has risen to 112 shillings and six pence (£5.62).

He was posted to N Bletchley in August, 1923, SW Wycombe October 1923 and SW Lane End in 1928 before being sent to Great Missenden on July 16, 1929.

In 1933 Sergeant Gubbins passed his qualifying exam for inspector but in the same year was severely reprimanded by Colonel TPR Warren, Chief Constable, for "neglect of duty by failing to make prompt enquiries into a report of larceny of fowls at Chalfont St Peter on the 11th March."

A keen horseman, following his police service Val went on to work as an inspector of diseases of animals for the London County Council and regularly checked the welfare of circus animals performing in the capital.

ERIC CHURCH

Eric Church was an experienced pilot who rejoined for RAF at the outbreak of the Second World War in 1939.

He had gained his wings previously during two years in the Volunteer Reserve.

Eric served during the war as a flight lieutenant in Coastal Command and was mentioned in dispatches for "valuable services in the air".

At the time of the crash he was 31 years old and had amassed more than 2,400 flying hours.

Born in Luton, Beds, where his father, Mr W Church, was a teacher at Luton Modern School, after the war he joined his brother-in-law, Roy Snelson, running Colwyn Motors, a taxi business in Babington Lane, Derby.

The business was sold two years later and Flt Lt Church rejoined the RAF Volunteer Reserve as an instructor, living in Byron Street, Derby.

He had married ten years earlier at Littleover Parish Church, Derby. The couple's son, Roger, was seven years old at the time of the crash.

WRAFVR FLYING BRANCH

Many women flew as ferry pilots with the Air Transport Auxiliary during the Second World War but the formation of a Women's Royal Air Force Flying Branch was only announced in 1947.

This was open to women aged 18 to 30 of British nationality who were qualified pilots with at least 100 hours solo.

They were required to undertake 15 days continuous training plus 130 hours weekend and evening training each year at RAF reserve centres and reserve training schools. This would include 20 hours flying in each phase.

Entrants were enrolled at NCO rank of Pilot IV and paid a flying training bonus and expenses. The target was 200 pilots, which was never reached. The first recruits were Margot Gore and Joan Naylor, both former ATA pilots. In July, 1952, four months after Barbara's death, it was agreed that WRAFVR pilots could be awarded the full RAF pilot's badge after passing the same flying and ground tests as male flying training school pupils.

A milestone in RAF history was reached on September 20, 1952, just six months after Barbara was killed, when Pilot Officer Jean Lennox Bird received her wings in a ceremony at No15 RFS at Redhill. Pilot Officer Lennox Bird died along with her two passengers on April 29, 1957, when the Miles Aerovan she was piloting crashed on takeoff from Manchester Ringway Airport.

The WRAFVR Flying Branch was closed in 1957. During its brief existence it had some 70 members of all ranks including 39 officers who were mostly former ATA pilots. It was a short-lived but exclusive club.

It was in 1994 that Flight Lieutenant Jo Salter became the first female operational fast jet pilot, flying Tornados with 617 Squadron, the Dam Busters.

PERCIVAL PRENTICE

The Percival Prentice is a basic trainer used by the Royal Air Force after the Second World War to replace the de Havilland Tiger Moth and Miles Magister.

It was unusual in having two seats side by side with dual controls and a third behind to give a second pupil "air experience".

PIGTAIL PILOT

The aircraft, which first flew on March 31, 1946, from the Percival factory at Luton Airport, Bedfordshire, was a low-wing monoplane with a fixed tailwheel undercarriage.

A number of modifications were carried out after trials to correct shortcomings in its handling characteristics. A total of 483 were built, some for India and Argentina.

The Prentice T1 had a wingspan of 46ft (14m) and was powered by a Gipsy Queen 32 6-cylinder, air-cooled inline engine producing 251 horsepower. This gave the aircraft a top speed of 143mph (230 kph).

It had a range of 396 miles (637 km) and a service ceiling of 18,000ft (5,490m). Its rate of climb was 653 feet per minute (3.3m/s). Its stall speed with flaps down was 56.6 mph (91km/h).

At the end of their service as a trainer in 1953 after just eight years about 250 were sold to Aviation Traders Ltd in Southend, Essex, a company owned by cheap flights pioneer Sir Freddie Laker. The aim was to sell them to private pilots.

They were given civilian registrations, converted to four-seaters and mostly painted silver grey before going on sale for £2,000. This was dropped to £1,500 but the Prentices were expensive to operate, underpowered in hot weather or with four aboard and guzzled fuel.

They were outsold by imported American rivals and most were dumped in heaps at Southend and Stansted and scrapped.

FATAL FLIGHT: This is a Hunting Percival Prentice T1 similar to the crash aircraft which carried the registration code VS 645

A handful survive including an airworthy Prentice owned by the Classic Air Force in Coventry and aircraft on static display at the RAF Museum, Hendon, Midland Air Museum and Newark Air Museum.

Norman Ellison's 1997 book on Percival aircraft says that during development the Prentice had "dismal spinning characteristics". This was improved by angling up the tips of the wings and fitting strakes to the fuselage and tail.

The website of the Coventry-based Classic Air Force says: "There's an unkind saying that the Prentice doesn't so much climb as trundle along the runway until the curvature of the Earth makes the ground fall away. There's no denying that she's a leisurely old bird with a distinct disapproval of rush but she's immensely strong, reliable and the cockpit is bigger than a London taxi."

It adds that the 1946 prototype was, "found to have inadequate yaw control, so later aircraft had a large rudder and cut-outs in the elevators to allow it to move further. In service it was also rare to have a crew of three due to performance limitations related to the 251hp Gipsy Queen engine."

RAF BURNASTON

RAF Burnaston was built on the site of the Burnaston House estate and the small grass airfield opened for training flights in 1938.

After the Second World War it became Derby Airport. Derby Aviation, which later became British Midland Airways, operated a number of scheduled flights, the first route being to Jersey in 1953.

Commercial flights ended at Burnaston in the 1960s when they transferred to the newly-opened East Midlands Airport nearby.

The airfield continued to be used by flying clubs until it closed in 1990. The site is now occupied by Toyota's vehicle assembly plant. The first car, a Carina E, drove off the Burnaston production line in 1992.

DENHAM

During the First World War the Royal Flying Corps used the airfield for training new pilots, flying Avros, RE8s and BE2Cs.

The airfield was closed at the start of the Second World War but reopened by the RAF after the fall of Dunkirk in 1940 and extended into a neighbouring golf course.

A fleet of 60 Tiger Moths and Magisters were used to train pilots and, later, for initial training for glider pilots. The intense activity attracted some 200 German bombs.

After the war the airfield was abandoned and suffered extensive damage and vandalism. Hundreds of tons of bomb rubble had been dumped there and scarce building materials were scavenged from the site.

In the 1950s proposals for the site included an estate for 2,000 houses, a gravel pit, a tip for London's rubbish, a mental hospital and even a prison.

But it survived as an airfield, now carrying the UN's International Civil Aviation Organisation identification code EGLD, and Denham Aero Club set up shop, flying mainly Miles Magisters and Austers.

At this time most training aircraft could perform basic aerobatics, as could the flying instructors, so learning to do a few simple loops and rolls was a normal part of training.

The pretty village of Denham was also home to the famous film studios. Founded by movie legend Alexander Korda in 1935, its famous films included Goodbye, Mr Chips (1939, Robert Donat), In Which We Serve (1942, Noël Coward, John Mills), Olivier's Henry V (1944), Brief Encounter (1945, Trevor Howard, Celia Johnson) and A Matter Of Life and Death (1946, David Niven).

Denham's last production was the Disney film The Story Of Robin Hood And His Merrie Men with Richard Todd in 1952. The site is now a business park.

WYCOMBE AIR PARK

Originally know as Marlow Airport, it became RAF Booker in the Second World War and from 1942 No21 Elementary Flying Training School taught new pilots using a fleet of 72 de Havilland Tiger Moths and Miles Magisters.

In May 1942, training began for the newly-formed Glider Pilot Regiment, teaching recruits to fly light aircraft.

They moved on to RAF Croughton in Northamptonshire for conversion to gliders and then RAF Brize Norton, Oxfordshire, to train on the heavier troop-carrying Airspeed Horsa gliders used in the D-Day landings and at Arnhem.

In July 1943 alone, trainees flew 5,576 hours, 442 of them at night.

In 1955, a hard runway was added to the four wartime grass runways. The RAF based its Bomber Command Communication Flight there until 1963 when the airfield was returned to private hands and became Wycombe Air Park with the ICAO identification code EGTB.

It was used for the films Those Magnificent Men In Their Flying Machines (1965, Terry-Thomas, Eric Sykes, Robert Morley) and Aces High (1976, Malcolm McDowell, Peter Firth).

PHOTO ALBUM

COURT SMILING: Barbara, front centre, in the first tennis team 1950

Hockey Teams	Autumn Term, 1949	
1st XI		2nd XI
Joan Bolton-King	G.K.	Patricia Hunter
Grace King	R.B.	Patricia Roberts
Barbara Gubbins (capt.)	L.B.	Pauline Brooking (capt.)
Janet Armstrong	R.H.	Betty Parker
Winifred Stevens	C.H.	Cicely Final
Barbara Pratchett	L.H.	Valerie Kipping
June Housden	R.W.	Greta Herbert
Anne Doble	R.I.	Patricia Poulter
Joan Arnold	C.F.	Heather Watson
Barbara Millidge	L.I.	Gwen Johnson
Christine Priest	L.W.	Doreen Glasson

STAR PLAYER: Barbara and the 1949 hockey team listed in the school magazine

PIGTAIL PILOT

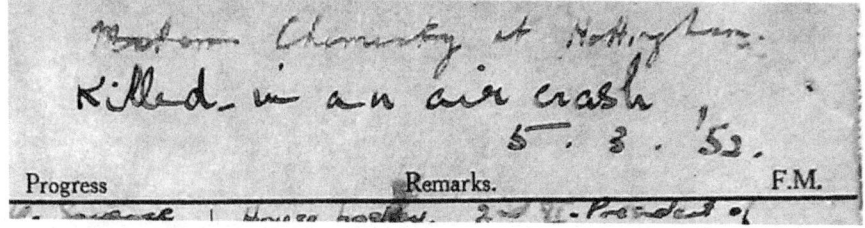

TEACHERS' VIEW: This densely-written report card charts the ups and downs of Barbara's progress in her last three years at Wycombe High School

LAST WORD: The brief annotation in the top right-hand corner of the report card above gives the bald facts of Barbara's short life after school

AIRBOURNE: A Percival Prentice T1 giving a pleasure flight at Kemble Airport, Gloucestershire, in 2007.

Picture: Arpingstone via Wikimedia

FAMILY OUTING: A day in the country. A smiling Barbara sits on the parapet of a bridge with her father Val on the left and her uncle Bill on the right. The woman on the left is Bill's wife Jean Gubbins (nee Poole) and the man is Leslie Todd, Bill's son-in-law. The picture is thought to have been taken in Chipping Warden, Northants, where the Gubbins trace their family back to 1600

HIGH CHURCH: The pretty parish church at Hedsor where Barbara's ashes are buried. It stands on a hill in the Chilterns overlooking the Thames. The nearby Wye Valley once powered many mills which were the main employers alongside local farms and two wharfs on the Thames. Writers Enid Blyton and Edgar Wallace once lived in the area

PIGTAIL PILOT

FLYING HIGH: A newspaper advert for the Percival Prentice trainer

PIGTAIL PILOT

BREAKING NEWS: The Scropton crash attracted extensive news coverage

PIGTAIL PILOT

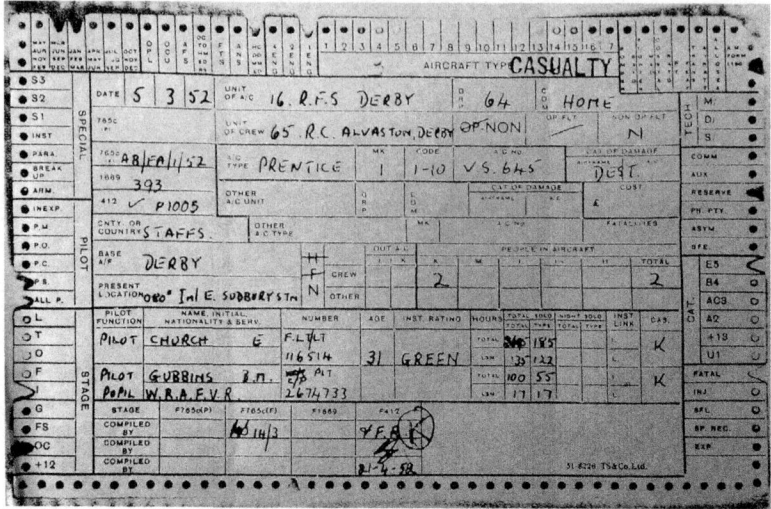

HARD FACTS: This is the report card for the RAF inquiry into the Scropton crash. It carries the barest details and some information is punched into pre-printed boxes around the edges. The cause was found to be, "a failure of the human element"

FINAL LANDING: The worn and weathered sandstone marker on Barbara's grave at Hedsor where all the stones are laid flat

PIGTAIL PILOT: This is the picture agency photo, taken on April 15, 1949, that gave this book its name. The caption reads, "Her heavy braids tucked beneath her flying helmet, Barbara Gubbins smiles confidently as she prepares to take off in a Miles Magister". The caption adds this is the first of five shots. The rest are lost to history

PIGTAIL PILOT

THANKS

In 2014 I had an email out of the blue from a French anthropologist in Croatia who collected helmets.

Pursuing his hobby on eBay, he'd found a photograph of Barbara in a flying helmet, Googled the name and got in touch through the website www.barbaragubbins.co.uk. I'd never seen the photo before. It was captioned "Pigtail Pilot" which gave this book its name.

The internet is home to many vices and dangers but it is also a miraculous tool for linking people who would never meet any other way.

I've attempted to weave a coherent story from patchy research sources, family stories, official documents, newspaper cuttings, websites and personal recollections.

I have tried not to make assumptions and any errors of transcription or interpretation are mine. But Pigtail Pilot would not have been possible without the time, knowledge and expertise of many kind and generous people.

This project started as a tribute website for the 60th anniversary of Barbara's death and has now grown into a book.

None of this would be possible without the help of many people including Ian Wallace, Rachel Sutcliffe of Wycombe High School Guild, flyer and air historian Pat Cunningham, author of *White Peak Air Crash Sites* (Amberley Books, price £16.99, ISBN 978-1-4456-0655-2), Rachel Butler of the Derby Telegraph, Buckinghamshire Constabulary historian Mick Shaw and Peter Elliott, Head of Archives at the Royal Air Force Museum Hendon. And not forgetting Eric Ripoll in Croatia.

Barbara's strength and enthusiasm helped her to achieve much in a handful of years. I can't help imagining, if that day over Scropton had ended differently, what might have been.

If anyone reading this has any more information about Barbara, please get in touch. My email address is: barbara2012@btinternet.com

Bill Todd, Hove, 2015

LINKS

Wycombe High School – www.whs.bucks.sch.uk
Hedsor Parish Church – www.stnicholashedsor.org.uk
Wycombe Air Park – www.wycombeairpark.co.uk
Denham Airfield – www.egld.com
Classic Air Force – www.classicairforce.com
Shuttleworth Collection – www.shuttleworth.org
RAF Museum Hendon – www.rafmuseum.org.uk
Bucks Constabulary – www.mkheritage.co.uk/bch/index.html
Guild Of One-Name Studies – http://one-name.org/name_profile/gubbins/
Bill Todd – www.billtodd.co.uk

THE AUTHOR

Bill Todd is a journalist and award-winning travel writer who has visited more than 40 countries from Arctic Finland to the deserts of Namibia. He enjoys Western Crete, maps, genealogy, military history, strong cheese and good beer. Bill is married with a daughter and lives in Hove and London.

In February 2015 Bill was voted one of the 100 best crime authors in the WH Smith readers' poll. Gargoyle Pixie Dog is his fifth Danny Lancaster crime thriller following The Wreck Of The Margherita, Death Squad, Rough Diamond and Rock.

He has also made an ebook from his father's World War Two diary, GUNNER.

Also published by DLE-History

Available at www.amazon.co.uk/dp/B00LGSZQTU.
All proceeds go to the Not Forgotten Association -
www.nfassociation.org @nfassociation

Coming soon...

The story of Corporal Frederick Gubbins who survived torpedo attack in the Mediterranean and went on to fight in the Middle East. He was killed in action in hand-to-hand fighting with the Ottoman Turks near Jerusalem at Christmas 1917.

PIGTAIL PILOT

DLE-Fiction publishes the DANNY LANCASTER series of crime novels in ebook and paperback

THE WRECK OF THE MARGHERITA – Where is the missing cargo?
When the Margherita sheds her load in a storm Danny Lancaster and his friends go beachcombing. But among the mangled containers they find more than they bargained for. That's when the real storm breaks.
- *"A good dose of gritty realism and strong dialogue"*
- *"A dark, sexy and intelligent novel"*

DEATH SQUAD – Who is murdering members of a 70s dinosaur rock band?
A "simple" surveillance job leads Danny to a gruesome discovery at the home of music legend Mickey "Tattoo" Carpenter. Suddenly Danny is wanted for murder. But that won't stop him hunting two hired killers.
- *"Great stuff, lots of bodice-ripping by bullet and basic instinct"*
- *"Action aplenty. Great stuff, packed with thrills and spills"*

ROUGH DIAMOND – What is the secret of Kaapse Kobra?
Marion Carter wants her husband. Jessie Shafto is looking for her lost love. It's two easy missing person jobs. But people who know the secret of a plane crash in Namibia have crossed the world for the Demon's Eye.
- *"A helter-skelter story of human emotion and family loyalty"*
- *"Plenty of sex, violence and humour"*

ROCK HARD – How far do you go to help the man who saved your life?
When Danny Lancaster gets a call from an old Army friend it looks like a chance for a sunshine reunion. But Pogo is broke, sick and in serious trouble with smugglers in Gibraltar. Unseen eyes are watching.
- *"Genuinely so much better than a lot of better known authors"*
- *"I could not put this down. Gripping, thrilling, entertaining"*

GARGOYLE PIXIE DOG – How do you find a girl who lives off the grid?
When young homeless street artist Cat goes missing her rough sleeper friend asks private investigator Danny Lancaster to find her. But how do you trace someone with no address, job, credit cards, no social media?
- *"A really enjoyable read. Danny is a great character."*
- *"Yet another blinder from the author."*

Printed in Dunstable, United Kingdom